D1361138

STEM IN FOOTBALL

SportsZone

An Imprint of Abdo Publishing
abdopublishing.com

BY BRETT S. MARTIN

ABDOPUBLISHING.COM
Published by Abdo Publishing, a division of ABDO, PO Box 398166, Minneapolis, Minnesota 55439.
Copyright © 2018 by Abdo Consulting Group, Inc. International copyrights reserved in all countries.
No part of this book may be reproduced in any form without written permission from the
publisher. SportsZone™ is a trademark and logo of Abdo Publishing.

Printed in the United States of America, North Mankato, Minnesota
092017
012018

THIS BOOK CONTAINS
RECYCLED MATERIALS

Cover Photo: Tony Gutierrez/AP Images
Interior Photos: Tony Gutierrez/AP Images, 1; Aaron M. Sprecher/AP Images, 4–5, 9; Jim Mahoney/
AP Images, 6; Michael Conroy/AP Images, 10; Ron Jenkins/AP Images, 12–13; Greg Trott/AP Images,
14, 17; Shutterstock Images, 14 (football); Keith Srakocic/AP Images, 19; Richard Lipski/AP Images,
20–21; LiPo Ching/Bay Area News Group/TNS/Newscom, 22; Rick Osentoski/AP Images, 24; Red
Line Editorial, 27, 42; Paul Spinelli/AP Images, 29; Chicago History Museum/Archive Photos/Getty
Images, 30–31; Bettmann/Getty Images, 33 (top); Ted Kinsman/Science Source, 33 (bottom); David
Banks/Getty Images Sport/Getty Images, 35; Roger Werth/The Daily News/AP Images, 36–37;
Marcio Jose Sanchez/AP Images, 38–39; Paul Sancya/AP Images, 41

Editor: Arnold Ringstad
Series Designer: Maggie Villaume
Content Consultant: Konstantinos Pelechrinis, Associate Professor, School of Computing and
      Information, University of Pittsburgh

PUBLISHER'S CATALOGING-IN-PUBLICATION DATA
Names: Martin, Brett S., author.
Title: STEM in football / by Brett S. Martin.
Description: Minneapolis, Minnesota : Abdo Publishing, 2018. | Series: STEM in sports | Includes
      online resources and index.
Identifiers: LCCN 2017946913 | ISBN 9781532113505 (lib.bdg.) | ISBN 9781532152382 (ebook)
Subjects: LCSH: Football--United States--Juvenile literature. | Sports sciences--Juvenile literature. |
      Physics--Juvenile literature.
Classification: DDC 796.332--dc23
LC record available at https://lccn.loc.gov/2017946913

Quarterback Tom Brady prepares to receive the snap from the center.

1

TACKLING FOOTBALL WITH STEM

It's a crisp autumn day. The crowd is whipped into a frenzy and cheerleaders are doing flips on the sidelines. The quarterback barks out the signals and the center snaps the ball, setting all 22 players on the field into motion. The players on the line of scrimmage collide with each other. Their protective gear makes crunching, popping, and smashing sounds.

Receiver Julian Edelman uses his gloves to help snag a touchdown pass.

Spikes in the receivers' shoes grip the turf, helping them accelerate. The quarterback drops back five steps and scans downfield. He spots his favorite receiver in the end zone. His arm muscles flex as he flings the ball in a fast, tight spiral. The ball's path takes an arc shape as it sails through the air 40 yards. The receiver times his jump perfectly, grabbing the ball out of the air.

The high-friction material used to make his gloves helps him pull in and secure the ball. Touchdown!

Science, technology, engineering, and math (STEM) play a role in all sports, including football. All of these concepts factor into success on the field. Knowing STEM can give a team a winning edge.

SCORING IN A GAME OF INCHES

Football is a unique sport. It has twenty-two players on the field, also called the gridiron. Eleven play offense, and eleven play defense. Positions are highly specialized. Some players never touch the ball.

The game brings together a variety of skills. Offensive linemen are big and strong to protect the quarterback from the defense. Receivers are tall and fast, and they make amazing catches. Running backs have powerful legs to run through tackles. Quarterbacks are agile, with strong arms to make long passes. Defenders tackle whoever has the ball. Each player has a job to do as soon as the ball is snapped.

The object of football is to advance the ball down the field and score as many points as possible while keeping the other team from scoring. Points are scored by a player running into the end zone or catching the football there. Teams also score by kicking the ball through upright posts in the end zone.

Football is sometimes called a game of inches. There are a lot of examples of players missing a touchdown or field goal by just a few inches. Such a small distance can make the difference between winning and losing. In this game of inches, players are always looking for any advantage to improve their level of play. That's where STEM can help.

STEM ON THE GRIDIRON

Because football has so many positions and types of plays, many aspects of STEM are on display in every game. Science helps players become more efficient with passing, catching, and running. Physics and laws of

With so many players on the field at one time, football players have a lot to keep track of during games.

motion determine the path the football takes when it's thrown, kicked, or fumbled.

Now more than ever, technology is a big part of the game. Players and coaches use tablet computers to review plays and formations during games. Wireless

Coaches use headsets and tablets to plan and communicate their strategy during games.

technology allows coaches to talk directly to players on the field.

In a full-contact, hard-hitting game like football, wearing the right gear is critical. Engineering creates helmets and pads that prevent injuries. In recent years, engineering has led to footwear, gloves, and clothing that improve performance.

Math is also important. Each player's statistics are tracked to measure his performance. When some players reach certain numbers, they earn hundreds of thousands of dollars in bonuses. Coaches also use stats and percentages to help with game strategy.

At every level of football, STEM is in play. It makes the game safer and more competitive, which also makes it more exciting to watch.

Throwing passes requires quick thinking and strong, precise movements.

2

THE SCIENCE BEHIND FOOTBALL

Science enables quarterbacks to achieve the most effective passing motion. Many scientists and kinesiologists agree that throwing the football is one of the most complex movements in all of sports. That's because mechanics, angles, alignment, timing, technique, and motion come together in a single action. Every part of the quarterback's body is used in a chain

AIR RESISTANCE

FORCE OF THROW
AT RELEASE

GRAVITY

During a throw, the quarterback's arm works like a lever. The faster the arm moves, the farther and faster the ball travels. Air is a force working against the ball, causing resistance, or friction. Momentum carries the ball through the air. When the ball is in motion, it has kinetic energy. Gravity pulls the ball downward, causing the ball to travel in an arc shape.

of events that ends with the ball heading toward a precise target.

Quarterbacks put a spin, or spiral, on the ball. The spiral gives the football angular momentum. The ball remains stable throughout its entire flight. It doesn't wobble in the air. The spiral gives the pass greater accuracy. Receivers can easily determine where the ball is going, so they can get there and make the catch.

FOOTBALL PHYSICS

When throwing a pass, the quarterback takes into account the distance to the receiver, the wind direction, and the weight of the ball. He does this very quickly, based on experience. The pattern a football takes when it's thrown is called a parabola. It starts on an upward path, then comes back down.

In physics, one of the laws of motion states that an object in motion, such as a football, will stay in motion unless an outside force stops it. Outside forces including air resistance and gravity impact the ball's path, slowing it and pulling it downward.

Another law of motion says if two objects collide they will exert opposite and equal forces. That explains the science behind a tackle. There are about 100 tackles during a pro game. A defensive back standing 5 foot 11 inches (180 cm) and weighing 200 pounds (91 kg) can produce 1,600 pounds (7,100 Newtons) of tackling force.

"DEFLATEGATE"

One of the biggest controversies in modern football was a playoff game in 2015, when the New England Patriots beat the Indianapolis Colts 47–7. Each team's offense provides its own footballs for the game. The Patriots were accused of cheating by letting air out of their footballs. The ensuing scandal became known as "Deflategate." It resulted in the Patriots facing several penalties.

The National Football League (NFL) has rules that specify the standard inflation and weight of footballs. Underinflated footballs are softer and easier to grip than fully inflated footballs. This makes the ball easier to hold onto, throw, and catch.

Big, heavy linemen collide with incredible force on almost every play.

Bill Belichick, the Super Bowl–winning head coach of the New England Patriots, described how science plays a role in football. "The action that happens on a football field involves mass, velocity, acceleration, torque, and many other concepts," he wrote in a book on football physics. "While some observers see only carnage and chaos, brilliant athletic performances, and bone-jarring collisions, the science-minded see the field as a working laboratory."

THE LOW MAN WINS

Coaches like to say "the low man wins" on the line of scrimmage. That's where offensive and defensive linemen, often weighing more than 300 pounds (136 kg) each, collide. Players look for any way to overpower their opponents. They get an advantage by keeping a low center of mass.

Every object, whether a person or thing, has a center of mass. When a force, such as a lineman pushing on a defender, is applied anywhere other than the center of mass, it causes the object to turn. A person's center of mass is just above the navel. If a player makes a tackle or a block below that area, it throws the other person off balance, causing him to slow down or fall.

PUNTING, KICKING, AND PROJECTILE MOTION

The path a ball takes from when it's kicked until it lands is called projectile motion. The kicker can control this motion by the angle of the kick, the ball rotation, and

Kickers and holders train to execute accurate, powerful kicks.

how fast the ball leaves his foot. These things determine the hang time, or how long the ball is in the air, and how high and far the ball will go.

Footballs kicked at a steep angle will go higher, but not as far, compared to kicks at shallow angles. Punters need to know what angle is needed to send the ball precisely where they want it.

On the field, the first down line is indicated by a sideline marker. On TV, viewers see a bright yellow line across the field.

3

FOOTBALL TECH

Technology affects how football is played, coached, and watched. In 1998, in a game between the Baltimore Ravens and the Cincinnati Bengals, the yellow first down line was introduced to TV viewers. The line is added to the field by computers. It is not visible in real life. The technology lets fans watching at home easily see how far the offense needs to go for a first down. People are so used to seeing the first-down line on their TVs that they forget it is computer generated. Some fans are surprised when

A user demonstrates a virtual reality training system.

they go to actual games and don't see the yellow marker on the field.

VIRTUAL TRAINING

A quarterback scans the field, trying to read the defense. He makes a signal, sending his tight end in motion. He calls out more signals, and then the ball is snapped. Dropping back a couple steps, he looks for an open receiver and throws a deep pass. This didn't happen in a game or practice. It happened within a virtual reality headset.

Football teams, from high school through the pros, are allowed a certain number of practices with tackling and blocking. The purpose of limiting practice time is to prevent injuries. With virtual reality, players can see game-type scenarios without an actual physical practice. This lets them train, learn, and improve without the risk of getting hurt.

BENEFITING FROM APPS AND VIDEOS

Watching game videos has long been an important part of preparing for games. Coaches can point out what worked or didn't work so players can learn. This used to be done by looking at camera film, then videotapes, then DVDs.

Now technology allows teams to watch streaming videos on TVs, computers, tablets, and smartphones. Software programs now let coaches write notes and

Tablets on the sidelines show stats and video to help players and coaches adjust their game plan.

attach them directly to plays. Even junior high school football teams use this technology.

As apps have become more popular, college football coaches use them for recruiting. When meeting with high school players, college coaches show off their program and highlights through an app. This puts all the

information at the student athlete's fingertips. Websites
also make it easier for college scouts to connect with
star high school players across the country.

PLAYER-FRIENDLY FOOTBALL FIELDS

Lambeau Field, where the Green Bay Packers
play, is called "the frozen tundra" because of the
Wisconsin city's bitterly cold temperatures. A famous
championship game between the Packers and the Dallas

COMPUTERS ON THE SIDELINES

Wireless technology is now commonplace on
sidelines. Teams used to look at black and white
printouts of plays. Now they see color images and
replays. Starting in 2014, the computer company
Microsoft began providing tablets specifically
built for football games. They can be used in the
blazing heat and the freezing cold. They can also
withstand rain and survive drops.

Coaches can draw on the tablets, make notes,
review plays, and zoom in on players. The tablets
provide images faster than printing out pictures.
In football, when seconds matter, making quicker
adjustments can be the difference between
winning and losing.

Cowboys in 1967 was nicknamed "The Ice Bowl" because it was played in subzero weather.

In many stadiums today, including Lambeau, the field itself doesn't actually get cold. That's because the playing field is heated. "It's just like playing in the summer on the grass," Packers offensive lineman T. J. Lang said in an interview. "It's never hard, it's never frozen."

Underground pipes filled with a liquid heat up the turf and prevent it from freezing. If the ground did freeze, it would become as hard as concrete. This would make the field unsafe, since players could get hurt when they're knocked to the ground.

NEW WAYS TO COMMUNICATE

Fans screaming, coaches yelling, officials blowing whistles, and music blaring through loudspeakers make games very loud. As a result, coaches and players have trouble hearing each other. The solution is

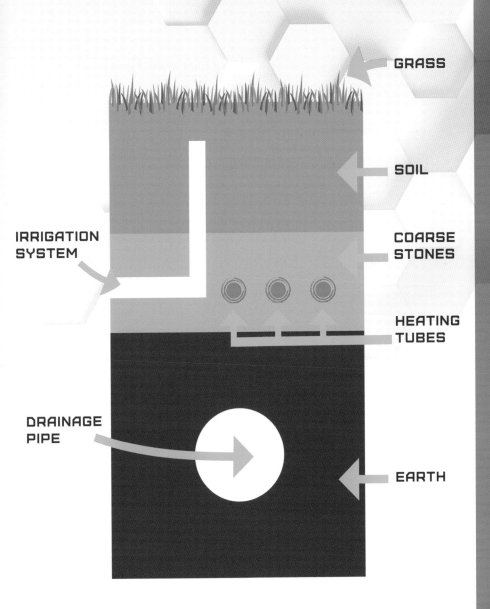

GRASS

SOIL

COARSE
STONES

IRRIGATION
SYSTEM

HEATING
TUBES

DRAINAGE
PIPE

EARTH

Heated athletic fields have heat conducted through pipes.
The pipes heat up the soil and grass, or in some cases
sand and turf, to keep the surface warm for players in
cold weather.

wireless communication, which allows everyone to talk through headsets.

Coaches, no matter where they are in the building, can talk and be heard clearly. Officials also wear headsets to talk with each other. This helps them determine the correct calls on plays and penalties, keeping the game moving faster.

During NFL games, the quarterbacks and one defensive player on each team wear special helmets. These helmets have a speaker in each ear hole, which allows the coaches to talk to the players. The wireless technology lets coaches call plays onto the field. Then the designated players share the information in the huddle.

New England Patriots coach Bill Belichick speaks on his headset.

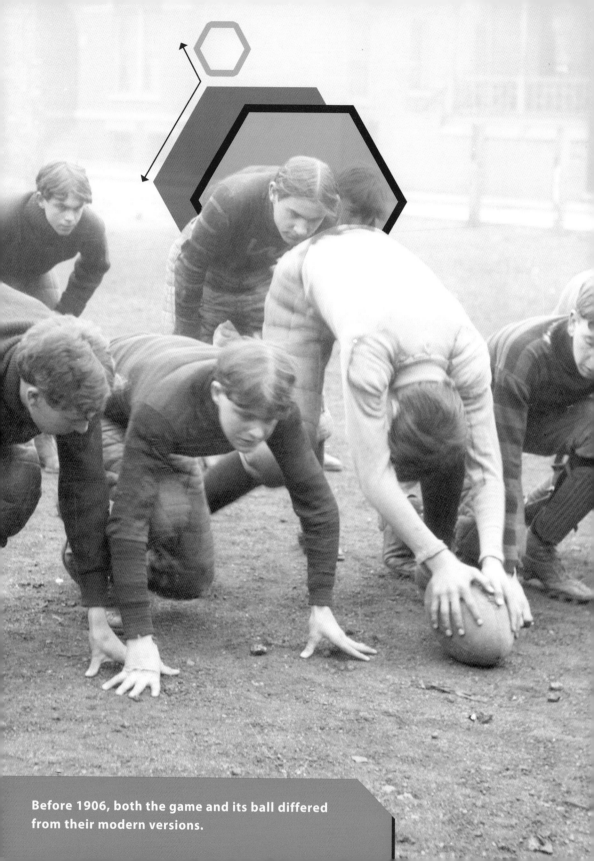

Before 1906, both the game and its ball differed from their modern versions.

4

ENGINEERING FOR SAFETY

A football is often referred to as a pigskin. That's because the first footballs were made from inflated pig bladders. Animal bladders were round, lightweight, easy to inflate, and durable.

The ball became wider in the center and skinnier on the ends in 1906, when the forward pass was allowed. The new shape allowed quarterbacks to better grip and throw it. The ball has continued to improve over the decades. Laces and texture were added to make it easier to hold and pass. The next change may be adding sensors inside the football. That would provide information to officials, letting them know, for example, if the ball actually crossed the goal line for a touchdown.

STRIVING FOR THE PERFECT HELMET

Despite safety efforts, injuries are still part of football. It's a hard-hitting game, and players often get hurt. One of the most serious injuries is a concussion. Improvements to safety gear and helmets have made the game much safer. However, no helmet can prevent all concussions.

New helmets also offer advanced engineering. Some have built-in sensors that measure impact. If a hit is too intense, a wireless alert is sent to a coach. This identifies players who may have a concussion.

Another option for helmets is built-in video cameras that can be used for coaching and broadcasting. The cameras would let fans see what players see.

FOOTBALL HELMET, 1925

FOOTBALL HELMET TODAY

Since the early days of football, engineers have worked to improve helmet design. The latest helmets are designed to help lessen the risk of concussions. They do that by dispersing energy during a tackle to reduce the impact to the brain. Layers of thick padding absorb some of the force of big hits before it reaches the brain.

The company behind the technology believes it will change the way fans watch football.

PROTECT PLAYERS WHILE ENHANCING ABILITIES

In addition to better helmets, other safety equipment has also improved. Shoulder pads, which protect the upper body, have become as much as 50 percent lighter during the last 15 years. New designs and materials have led to the improvements. Carbon fiber is now used. This material is strong, yet lighter than the materials used before. It reduces the force of a hit felt by the player

ENGINEERING IN ACTION

CLOTHING ADVANCES

Clothes that absorb shock are important in a contact sport such as football. The clothes, called padded or shock-resistant gear, have extra padding. The shirts have foam padding over the ribs and shoulders to protect the bones during a tackle.

In the last few years, shirts that pull sweat away from the body have become popular across all sports. These shirts are made with polyester, which is durable and lightweight. This modern fabric helps players stay cool without wearing clothing that is damp and uncomfortable.

Today's football pads are lightweight yet protective.

by 63 percent. This allows smaller, lighter, and more comfortable gear that offers more protection.

MOUTH GUARDS DO MORE THAN PROTECT TEETH

Mouth guards keep a player's teeth from being damaged. They are also believed to protect against

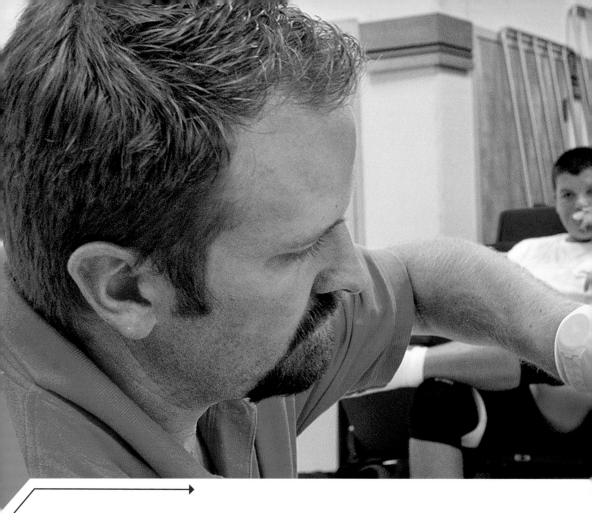

concussions, especially when custom-made by a dentist to precisely fit a player's mouth.

One study found that high school football players wearing store-bought mouth guards were more than twice as likely to get a concussion as players wearing custom mouth guards. One reason is that

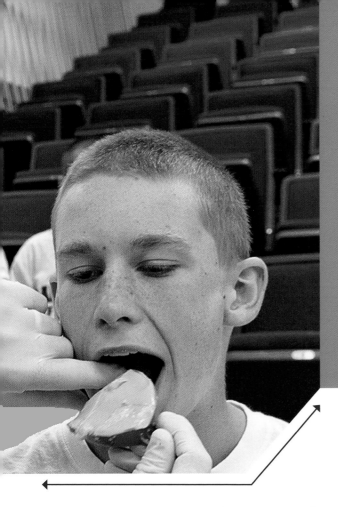

A doctor inserts a mold into a high-school player's mouth in order to create a customized mouth guard.

custom mouth guards are more than twice as thick as over-the-counter models.

Newly engineered mouth guards have sensors that monitor a player's saliva. The sensors can detect if the player is injured or tired. Another company has created a mouth guard with a sensor that tells if the player has taken a hit that might have caused a concussion.

In fantasy football, every thrilling play is translated into statistics that fans track carefully.

CHAPTER **5**

A GAME OF NUMBERS

In the game of fantasy football, fans pick a dream team of their favorite players. Those players' statistics count as points for the fantasy teams. The fan with the highest-scoring team wins. Fantasy versions of many sports are wildly popular. They are based on math and statistics.

Fantasy players are obsessed with statistics to determine which players to put on their rosters. The NFL has taken notice. Its own website allows fans to build and manage fantasy teams. The league is also finding ways to create even more new statistics. It has added sensors to players' shoulder pads. This wearable technology offers details about the speed, distance, and direction players travel in a game.

EVERYTHING COMES DOWN TO NUMBERS

In football, the offense gets four plays to move the ball at least 10 yards to make a first down. As long as the offense keeps making first downs, it keeps the ball. Math determines the distance needed to gain a first down. Sometimes, that's just a few inches.

Coaches want to know which players and plays are most likely to get the required yards in specific situations. They rely on statistics for that information. For example, when a team needs just one yard, a quarterback sneak might statistically be the best play. On that play, the quarterback takes the snap and plows forward behind the center. The quarterback sneak works

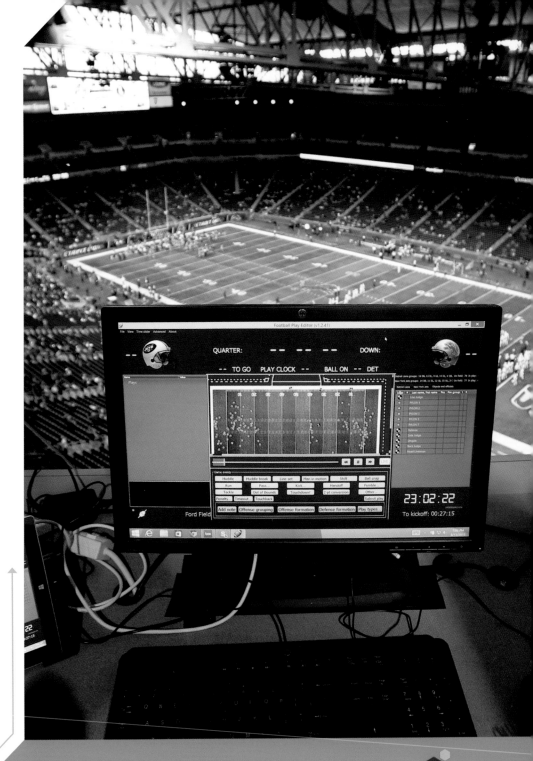

Each game generates enormous amounts of new statistics and data that help teams improve.

$$(\text{completion percentage} - 30) \times 0.05 = \mathbf{A}$$

$$(\text{yards per attempt} - 3) \times 0.25 = \mathbf{B}$$

$$(\text{touchdown percentage}) \times 0.2 = \mathbf{C}$$

$$2.375 - [(\text{interception percentage}) \times 0.25] = \mathbf{D}$$

$$\frac{\mathbf{A} + \mathbf{B} + \mathbf{C} + \mathbf{D}}{6} \times \mathbf{100} = \text{QUARTERBACK RATING}$$

A quarterback rating is based on four categories. They are percentage of completions per pass attempt, average yards gained, percentage of touchdown passes, and percentage of interceptions. This lets teams and fans compare quarterbacks based solely on their stats.

The quarterback rating is based on math. The rating is on a scale from 0 to 158.3. The rating system measures four categories, but other factors such as rushing yards and leadership are not included. The system is not perfect because a quarterback's rating goes down if he purposely throws the ball out of bounds to avoid a sack, even though that's a good decision. Still, the rating allows all quarterbacks to be compared using the same criteria.

82 percent of the time. Having the running back run the ball is only successful on 66 percent of those plays.

STATISTICALLY PREPARED FOR GAMES

Statistics help teams prepare for games by telling coaches the plays opponents are likely to run. Coaches want to know how often a team runs to one side of the field, if the quarterback is more likely to pass in certain situations, and other details. For example, statistics let coaches know which receiver is most likely to catch a deep pass, which defender is best at stopping the run, and what plays to run on a third down when they need just two yards. This helps coaches make better decisions when calling plays.

ANALYZING THE DATA

One debate in football is if a team should try to make a first down if it only needs a couple yards on fourth down, or play it safe and punt. Punting gives the ball to the other team, but it can pin them deep on the other side of the field. If the offense tries for the first down and fails, the other team gets the ball at that spot. If the play is successful, the offense keeps the ball and continues the drive.

In college and especially in the NFL, conventional wisdom says to punt. However, some statistics suggest teams should be going for it on fourth down more often.

MATH IN ACTION

STATISTICS PROMPT RULE CHANGES

Analyzing football stats sometimes leads to rule changes. Holding, illegal use of the hands, and tripping by the offense used to trigger 15-yard penalties. They were reduced to 10 yards after statistics showed that teams rarely made a first down or scored after being moved back 15 yards. Most recently, the NFL changed a rule for kickoffs. If the kick goes into the end zone, the receiving team has the option of catching the ball and running it out, or taking a knee. The team taking a knee used to get the ball at the 20-yard line. Starting in 2015, the receiving team gained an extra five yards, getting the ball at the 25-yard line. The purpose was to encourage teams to take a knee and settle for the satisfactory field position. This was designed to reduce the number of teams running the ball out of the end zone, in turn reducing the number of tackles and injuries.

For instance, if a team is on the opponent's 37-yard line and needs three yards for a first down, it might attempt a long field goal if it has a strong kicker. One study suggests that the average NFL team has a better chance of making a first down in that situation than of making the field goal.

As any player, coach, and football fan knows, all of the best data and information can't predict everything that can happen on game day. No one can predict a receiver making an incredible leap and plucking the ball out of the air for a game-winning touchdown. Data can't tell if a field-goal kicker will miss an easy kick that costs the team the game. But STEM concepts can give teams and players an edge. They can make the game safer, more exciting, and more fun to watch. Every time they take the field, football players and coaches are putting STEM principles into action.

GLOSSARY

CONCUSSION

An injury to the brain as the result of a violent blow or collision, such as a hard tackle or a player hitting his head on the ground.

KINESIOLOGIST

A person who studies anatomy, physiology, and the mechanics of body movement, especially in humans.

MOMENTUM

The quantity of motion of a moving body, measured as a product of its mass and velocity.

PARABOLA

A symmetrical curve formed by an object's motion.

SENSOR

A device that detects or measures a physical property and records it, indicates it, or otherwise responds to it.

SNAP

To pass the ball back to the quarterback at the beginning of a play.

VIRTUAL REALITY

An immersive environment created by a computer and often viewed through a headset.

ONLINE RESOURCES

Booklinks
NONFICTION NETWORK
FREE ONLINE NONFICTION RESOURCES

To learn more about STEM in football, visit
abdobooklinks.com. These links are routinely monitored and
updated to provide the most current information available.

MORE INFORMATION

BOOKS

Slingerland, Janet. *Sports Science and Technology in the Real World*. Minneapolis, MN: Abdo Publishing, 2017.

St. John, Allen, and Ainissa Ramirez. *Newton's Football: The Science Behind America's Game.* New York: Ballantine Books, 2013.

Wilner, Barry. *Total Football*. Minneapolis, MN: Abdo Publishing, 2017.

INDEX

ABOUT THE AUTHOR

Brett S. Martin has more than 20 years of writing experience. He has written several fiction and nonfiction books. He has also volunteered as a youth football coach for nine seasons. Martin lives in Shakopee, Minnesota, with his wife and two teenage sons.